PRAISE FOR
EVAN BRAIN!

Oh my lord, I just received it and read it. It's fabulous!
Tell Evan that it's possible to overthrow the evil overlords of education.
He just has to get more subversive and a lot more quiet. That's ok, don't
tell him. I'll just mail him a kit.

—Deven Karpelman, middle school teacher, Bothell, WA

Evan is a very distinct character with a cockeyed/
sometimes villainous view of the world.

—Steve Moore, Cartoonist, "In the Bleachers", Universal Press Syndicate

First of all, I must say the illustrations seem PERFECT!
I just loved them and feel they added a lot to the story.
This seems to me like a juvenile fiction piece because of the vocabulary,
as well as all the imaginative, sci-fi sounding titles
given to the characters in Evan's version of the story.

—Patty Kimmel, kindergarten teacher, Clarksville, TN

I really like that story. It was funny and the
drawings were cool. Please write another one.

—Rachel S., age 8, Waterbury, VT

EVAN BRAIN! is creatively whimsical. What a cute story and great
visuals as well. The story reminded me (and my son Drew, 11 years old next
month) of one of his favorite online books: Diary of a Wimpy Kid.

—Morton Gernsbacher, PhD, Professor of Sociology/Psychology,
University of Wisconsin, Madison

I am in stitches.

—John Baffa, PhD, Associate Professor of English, Morton Community College, Elmhurst, IL

I liked the book. It was interesting and funny. I liked the pictures and the
parts about Calvin and Hobbes. The letters were funny! Can I keep the book?

—Tyler Walker, 10, Anaheim, CA

MORE PRAISE....

I just read your manuscript. Fantastic! I thought it was great and I LOVED the drawings! I actually laughed out loud while reading it. Tell Evan to remember me when he's rich and famous. Maybe I should go ahead and get his autograph now before the handlers and groupies converge.

—Stephen Young, Executive Director, Leukemia Texas, Dallas, TX

I think EVAN BRAIN! is great. Don't forget us little people when you are famous and win all those awards.

—Robert Kersey, PhD, Professor, Cal State Fullerton, Fullerton, CA

Hilarious! God bless Evan! He and his antics kept me going! I had a good laugh, and it's wonderful reading. If Calvin were real, Evan could outdo him!

—Linda Baird, Aflac salesperson, Dallas, TX

That was great!

—Nathaniel Hannon, 10, London, Ontario, Canada

I love the idea and the project. I see this as appealing to a young adult audience. I think it is extremely witty and creative – suited to the middle school person – I see some of my 8th grade Pre AP Literature students loving this! The combination of the more mature humor, drawings, and fantasy/science fiction orientation makes it an attraction to the adolescent kid. They are still young enough to understand and appreciate their experiences at a younger age. Also, the illustrations are quite good!

—Vivian Toole, 8th grade English teacher, Bishop Lynch, Dallas, TX

I enjoyed reading your book! I really liked the artwork! And the terrific descriptions of "fantasy" (I know better) creatures! And the pithy descriptions of Evan's Evil Parents! How does he put up with them?! And his teachers! Makes me think of Sister Mary Frumentia from fifth grade! And she was no fantasy creature – but she could have been! Keep up the great work! And the exclamatory punctuation!!

--Richard Ray, EdD, Professor, Hope College, Holland, MI

EVE'S DEDICATION

To Evan, my son who marches to the beat
of his own drummer, with love, and for my father,
Bryan Becker, who would have been so proud.

EVE'S ACKNOWLEDGMENTS

Thanks to my wonderful spouse Barry Doyle
and the many folks who collaborated, edited,
encouraged and believed in me and this project:
Karen Peterson, Nancy Tillman, Rachael
Oates, Caroline Hatton, Teresa Foster Welch,
Patti Kimmel, Tory Doyle, Cate Brennan
Lisak and Paula Duckworth.

Introducing Evan "Brain" Doyle, age 15, forced against his will by his cruel mother to write and illustrate this book

Parents will enjoy the wit and understated humor of Evan's longsuffering mother, Eve Becker-Doyle. *Evan didn't lack for brains, although his father pointed out he didn't put them to good use much*…she describes Evan's unfortunate encounters with educators, babysitters and family members whose patience is pushed to the limit. Whether you're 8 or 80, you'll love Evan's hilarious antics and stunts.

Kids will revel in Evan's fantasy accounts of each story, chock-full of a bizarre cadre of creatures and characters … Orphax Jackalopes that jump around the backyard like popcorn … a kindergarten teacher known as the evil hag Torblaz Mugtulla … another evil hag who wants to stew Evan in the juices of a Garblaxian Fireworm … evil overlord principal who allows Evan the kid to enjoy a three-day vacation.

★ ★ ★

day job, Eve Becker-Doyle is CEO of the National Athletic Trainers' Association. With an endless supply of Evan she foresees more **EVAN BRAIN!** books, and has ped a line of irreverent **EVAN BRAIN!** greeting and oliday cards (www.evanbrain.com).

Evan Brian Doyle is enrolled in the Dallas Public Schools. He graduated from Travis Talented and Gifted Middle School and now maintains an undistinguished academic career at the Science and Engineering Magnet High School.

His interests are computers, comics and sleeping. He does not care for writing books; his mother makes him.

Becker Doyle & Associates Publishing, Dallas, TX

At last–a real successor to Calvin and Hobbes! Evan Doyle is a truly gifted cartoonist. His work is fresh, witty and edgy–with a diverse cast of endlessly delightful, wickedly funny characters. I only wish Evan's work was in my daily paper so that I could have the pleasure of following his adventures every day.

Nicholas Gilroy, PhD, Professor Emeritus of Communication, Bronx Community College of the City University of New York

Evan's point of view is slightly different from a normal person's point of view. And that is what makes this book a magnificent choice for readers of all ages.

Katie F. Welch, 11, Dallas, TX

U.S. $13.95
ISBN: 978-0-9794716-0-5
5 1 3 9 5

EVAN BRAIN!

adventures of a delusional kid superhero

HEY LADIES.

written by
Eve Becker-Doyle
and
Evan "Brain"
Doyle

illustrated by
Evan "Brain" Doyle

EVAN BRAIN!

Library of Congress Cataloging-in-Publication Data available
LCCN: 2007902887

ISBN-13: 978-0-9794716-0-5
ISBN-10: 9794716-0-5

Becker Doyle & Associates Publishing
Dallas
October 2007
www.evanbrain.com

Book design by Peri Poloni-Gabriel,
Knockout Design, www.knockoutbooks.com

Printed in Canada

EVAN BRAIN!

adventures of a delusional kid superhero

TABLE OF CONTENTS

THE INSIDER'S GUIDE TO
EVAN BRAIN!

Here's what you need to know to figure out EVAN BRAIN!

This book contains two versions of each chapter.

★ Eve wrote the chapters labeled "According to Eve." Each story about Evan's escapades is basically true, and includes Evan's original notes, schoolwork assignments and communications from disgruntled teachers.

★ Evan wrote his own imaginative fantasy version of each chapter. It's not hard to see which one is Evan's because his are labeled "According to Evan."

★ Evan did all the illustrations in the book, although he claims he can't draw. Evan is 15.

★ Eve really can't draw. She's a grown-up.

CHAPTER 1

EVAN BRAIN *and His Family*

... *according to Eve*

Evan was a unique and unusual boy. As a kid superhero, he looked at the world differently than other children do. He liked to be original.

Evan did not trouble himself much with doing homework. What was the point of that?

One assignment he didn't mind too much. It was about his family. A very strange group of people lived in his house. This was probably something he couldn't keep secret much longer.

So Evan ratted on them. About his parents Evan wrote:

Family member's name	Four words to describe this person	Three things this person loves	Two things this person needs	One thing this person fears	One thing this person wishes
Barry	weird gigantic scary funny	my mom his computer cooking	a Corvette new pots and pans	roaches	everybody was like my mom
Eve	peaceful hardworking cruel odd	her work my dad radios	a TV a new car	TV	there weren't any TVs

Besides his parents, Evan had noticed two other people lived at his address. One was a boy, whom his mom and dad claimed was his brother. And there was a girl too, who supposedly was his sister.

Evan knew better. He was certain they couldn't be related to him. Evan couldn't think of one good reason a kid superhero needed a sister or a brother.

About his brother and sister Evan wrote:

Family member's name	Four words to describe this person	Three things this person loves	Two things this person needs	One thing this person fears	One thing this person wishes
Colin	tall strong mean hilarious	bicycles food his girlfriends	a heart less girlfriends	his girlfriends dumping him	that he had more girlfriends
Tory	slow large girly annoying	her bedroom Brad Pitt "Friends"	a life a new bedroom	everything	she had a new bedroom

The teacher said Evan had to be part of the family portrait. He was happy to write a few lines about himself. He knew he was from this family. But he wasn't sure where his brother and sister came from. And he didn't really care.

This is what Evan had to say about Evan.

HEY LADIES...

Family member's name	Four words to describe this person	Three things this person loves	Two things this person needs	One thing this person fears	One thing this person wishes
Evan	cool smart funny muscley	The Simpsons math science	telekinetic powers more books	spiders	I was a forensic pathologist

Eve's version of EVAN BRAIN and His Family ends here.

Here's how EVAN BRAIN's brain saw his "family"...

EVAN BRAIN *and His Family*

The Other Side of the Story… according to Evan

Evan had always known that a group of mindless Venusians had stolen the identities of his family. He would now divulge the secret to the public through this school assignment.

Besides his parents, Evan observed two other freakish alien beings living in his house. One was a boy, obviously a Zargaxian Gortak from a distant galaxy. His parents claimed that this gruesome creature was Evan's brother. There was a girl as well. She, too, was an imposter— a Tentacle-eyed Bloodworm from the Sulfuric Mudpits of Rigel IV. A hideous creature, indeed.

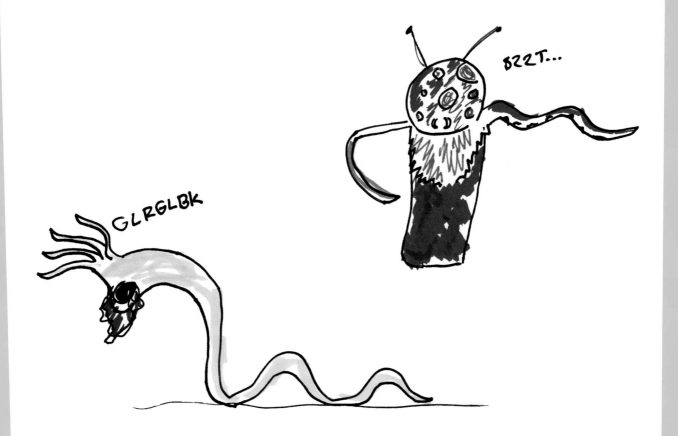

The creatures were obviously not related to him. They did not possess any redeeming qualities.

The evil overlord called teacher decreed Evan had to be part of this thing called a family portrait.

Evan was always ready to write about himself and it was a relief to write about someone attractive, rather than describing bubbly-skinned poop-hued creatures that had a tendency to howl at bad times.

CHAPTER 2

EVAN BRAIN *and the Comics*

... according to Eve

Evan liked to read comics. No other reading material interested kid superheroes much. He identified with the naughty characters. They reminded him of someone.

His mother thought the comics were a bad influence. She claimed they were the cause of his shenanigans.

Shenanigans were what you did when you were naughty.

His mother often bought Evan books she was sure he would like. He didn't read them. If she made him read a few chapters, he always said the book was stupid. He might have read a real book once in a while, but reading one his mother had suggested was out of the question.

His father said comics were better than TV.
Evan figured this might be one thing his father was right about.

When Evan visited his grandmother, they often ran into her neighbors roaming the hallways of her retirement apartment. The old ladies would ask, "This the one that's got the devil in him?"

Since his grandmother never denied it, Evan tried to play the part. He strained to make his ears pointy, which is not so easy, and think evil thoughts, which is not so hard. After a while he realized this was a meaningless exercise, since the old birds didn't see well enough to know if he had horns or a tail.

According to his grandmother, Evan was the reincarnation of Dennis the Menace. That wasn't right.

YOU'RE JUST LIKE DENNIS THE MENACE!

PREPOSTEROUS!

Dennis was at least a million years old, and besides, Evan was way cooler than Dennis.

It was Calvin whom Evan identified with. Evan was sure he had been Calvin before being sent to earth as a kid superhero. On his birthday Evan got a stuffed Hobbes. Most of the time, at least when grownups were around, Hobbes sat quietly on the bed.

This is the end of Eve's version of EVAN BRAIN and the Comics.

Meanwhile, in EVAN BRAIN's brain, it happened this way...

EVAN BRAIN *and the Comics*

The Other Side of the Story…according to Evan

Evan liked chasing the Orphax Jackalopes in his backyard. The Orphax Jackalopes didn't smell too bad.

No other type of animal chasing interested him much. He thought the way the Orphax Jackalopes jumped and darted around the yard was cool. It reminded him of popcorn.

His mother said the Jackalope-chasing scared the Jackalopes and was a bad thing. But Evan knew the Jackalopes wanted to be chased. It was a game, not a shenanigan.

Shenanigans were what you did when you were bad.

When Evan visited his grandmother, they often ran into her neighbors roaming the hallways of her retirement apartment. The old ladies would invariably ask, "This the good-smelling one?"

Since his grandmother never denied it, Evan tried to play the part. Before going to visit, he splashed strong cologne, eau de carcass, under his arms, which is easy if you don't mind the smell, and sprinkled eau de gross on his knee caps, which is not so hard.

After a while he realized this was a meaningless exercise, since the old birds couldn't smell well enough to know if he was the Bulgari poster boy or Walter the Farting Dog.

According to his grandmother, Evan was the reincarnation of Dennis the Menace. That wasn't right. Dennis was a weakling, and couldn't snap the neck of an Ixzam Toadstool if his life depended on it.

It was the pangalactic gladiator, Ulgrog the Footstomper, whom Evan identified with. The gladiator was known to complain and have a bad attitude. Occasionally this behavior was accompanied by the stomping of his left foot. At times Evan was sure he had been Ulgrog the Footstomper before being assigned to earth as a kid superhero.

On his birthday, Evan smelled too good to do anything except open his presents. He got a stuffed mascot just like the real one belonging to Ulgrog the Footstomper.

CHAPTER 3

EVAN BRAIN *and His Kindergarten Teacher*
... according to Eve

Some of the time Evan thought school was okay, but Evan didn't take much notice of the rules.

His teachers noticed he didn't take much notice. They didn't seem to like this.

Evan's father didn't like it much either.

In school, teachers write notes. At least Evan's teachers did. The notes were always addressed to his mom and dad. Most people like getting messages and letters, but not his parents.

Evan's kindergarten teacher wrote a nice note on his report card.

Six Week Period: 1 ② 3   4   5   6

Teacher Comments: *Evan is really putting forth an effort to improve on his work habits! His respect for others is improving also. Thanks*

Parent Comments: *for the support!*

Evan's dad commented that Ms. M had a positive outlook on life.

Evan liked Ms. M. But he didn't hold a high opinion of Ms. M having a baby and leaving school after first semester. He didn't like the substitute much either. She didn't appreciate kid superheroes.

Evan thought the rounded part of each shoe that covered his toes looked the same. He wasn't sure how other people could tell their shoes apart. Since there didn't seem to be a wrong foot, Evan put his shoes on whichever foot was handy.

The substitute asked his father if Evan could wear his shoes on the right foot. Evan heard his father mutter they wouldn't both fit on the right foot. It seemed the substitute was not a fan of individual expression.

One day Evan and his friend were playing under the computer table with some scissors. Evan cut his friend's hair, and the friend cut the computer cable.

The substitute teacher got a headache and went home. She didn't come back.

Too bad.

Apparently the principal had a headache as well, because Evan got to go home too…for three days.

Now Evan could see what Hobbes got up to during the day when he was usually at school.

Eve's version of EVAN BRAIN and His Kindergarten Teacher ends here.

This is what EVAN BRAIN'S brain thought about life in kindergarten...

EVAN BRAIN *and His Kindergarten Teacher*

The Other Side of the Story… according to Evan

In prison (also known as school), the evil hags, or teachers, have an obnoxious tendency to write things called notes. Or, at least, Evan's hags did. The notes, addressed to his mom and dad, contained devious plans relayed from the mothership.

Evan liked Evil Torblax Mugtulla (her human name was Ms. M), but he didn't hold a high opinion of her having a baby and leaving him in prison after the first semester. Evan also didn't much care for the thought of aliens reproducing.

ARENʼT THEY DARLING?

One day, Evan was violently attacked by a dim-witted Gorbat, in the form of an ugly child.

The Gorbat had in its possession a pair of knives, and forced Evan under a set of computer tables. A titanic fight ensued. Computer cables were cut during the vicious brawl, and Evan succeeded in scalping the Gorbat alive. The Gorbat fled.

The new evil hag fled as well, obviously intimidated by Evan's prowess with a blade. She never returned.

Too bad.

Due to his victory against the Gorbat, the evil overlord known as the principal allowed Evan to have a three-day vacation.

Now he could finish his surveillance on his unwitting parents.

CHAPTER 4

EVAN BRAIN *and His First Grade Teacher*

...according to Eve

Evan didn't lack for brains, although his father pointed out he didn't put them to good use much. Evan knew he was smart. His middle name was Brian, but sometimes he wrote "Evan Brain" on his school papers.

This annoyed his first grade teacher, Ms. H, which was part of the point. Usually he didn't put any name on his school work...when he turned it in, that is. That annoyed Ms. H even more.

Ms. H was a good teacher. Evan had noticed she didn't seem to have as positive an outlook on life as his kindergarten teacher. She was grumpy.
Ms. H wrote notes too, just like in kindergarten. This year Evan also got to write notes.

A note was sent home before long.

Dear mom and Dad,

I Threw away 10 peices of work and
I was playing today and talking today

Sincealy,
Evan

This did not make Evan's father happy. He didn't like getting the note Ms. H sent home a few days later either.

> *Evan hit Nicholas Rivers. Evan at times has an attitude problem. I speak to his father on an almost daily basis.*

Evan's parents said when you do something that's not nice, you have to do something nice to make it up to that person. One way to do this was to send an apology note. Evan was getting lots of practice writing that he was sorry. He was getting good at it.

> Dear   Mrs.H
>
> I   am   sorry   that   I   have been   hiting   and   kicking   people this   week. I   will   not   do   it   again.
>
>   Sinceraly,
>   Evan

His mother thought "Insincerely, Evan" was more like it.

MORE GRR

As the school year went on, Ms. H seemed to be getting grumpier…if that was possible.

She wrote this note to his parents.

> Mr. and Mrs. Doyle,
>   If this behavior continues after spring break, you will be called to sit with Evan. I can not allow this in class. Today he acted like a bully toward two different individuals. This will not be tolerated.
>
>   Sincerely,
>   Ms. H

Evan's father was not pleased. He said he'd already been to first grade, and once was enough.

Eve's version of EVAN BRAIN and His First Grade Teacher ends here.

EVAN BRAIN'S brain had a different perspective on first grade...

EVAN BRAIN *and His First Grade Teacher*
The Other Side of the Story…according to Evan

The next year, Evan's evil hag went by the name Ms. H. She lived up to her title as an evil hag. She was green, breathed through her eyes, and, just like the previous hags, she continued to relay secret encoded messages to Evan's parents. For some dumb reason, she made Evan write some of the notes as well.

Dear Mom and Dad,

I received ten lashes today for enjoying myself.

Sincerely,

Evan

Soon afterwards, the evil hag got off her lazy derriere and wrote a note herself. Evan caught a glimpse of it, and it took only a moment to decipher.

Mr. and Mrs. Doyle,

The mothership is nearing completion of our goals. Soon the solar system will be ours. MWAAAHAHAHAHAHA! MWAAAHAHAHA!

Ms. H

Evan's parents said when you do something that's not nice, you must endure sixty-three lashes for seven cycles. An alternative is to send an apology note. Evan thought it was a freakish custom. Obviously his parents were ripening his hand-flesh for eating.

Dear evil hag,

Do your worst.

Sincerely, Evan

His mother suggested signing his notes with "Q'waplagh!" might be more accurate. Evan had no idea what she was talking about.

As the year in prison went on, the evil hag seemed to become more and more evil and haggy. She wrote this easily-deciphered note to his parents.

Mr. and Mrs. Doyle,

You infidels! The mothership must beam aboard your youngling for preparation for consumption and yet you refuse?! I will have your heads on my mantle by the time this cycle has ended!

Ms. H

CHAPTER 5

EVAN BRAIN *and His Second Grade Teacher*

...according to Eve

Evan got to have the same teacher for second grade too. He wasn't that excited when he found out. Evan's father said Ms. H probably wasn't excited about it either.

Evan wondered if Ms. H had missed writing his parents over the summer. It didn't take long for her to get back into the habit.

> Some of Evan's report grades will reflect this problem. Also, Mrs. W. has been having quite a bit of trouble from Evan in the library lately. I will not be able to send him to the library to finish research work until I see an improvement.
>
> Ms. H

That was okay. Evan liked going to the library, but he didn't care about doing research work, whatever that was.

THAT STUPID KID!

NOTE

A few days later Ms. H said it was Evan's turn to write a note. Evan didn't want to write a note. When he did, it sounded kind of rude.

Evan was a good speller, especially for a second grader. His teacher said Evan's recalcitrance is what made his spelling in the note so poor.

Evan didn't know he had any of that. He figured out from his dictionary that recalcitrant is when someone makes you do something you don't want to, and you're not very happy about it.

note for my behaveyur.
Dear DaD and mom,

I hit nathyul and ANDrew in the hall. I hit nathanyul befor lunch, and i hit ANDrew after lunch so I coulD not have a chanch to write this note.

sinsilre your
son
evan

The following week Ms. H wrote his parents again. This note was special because it was on pink paper. It was called a "referral". A referral was not something you wanted to take home to your parents, even if you were a kid superhero. It told more than they needed to know.

TEACHER REFERRAL

Evan hit Nathaniel in class because Nathaniel accidentally touched him when scooting over. Evan has been out of control all week. He's hit others, not listened and been disruptive in class.

Ms. H

Turns out Evan's parents didn't like notes on pink paper. Evan figured Calvin had probably gotten a referral or two.

Eve's version of EVAN BRAIN and His Second Grade Teacher ends here.

As EVAN BRAIN's brain saw it, here's the story on second grade...

EVAN and *His Second Grade Teacher*

The Other Side of the Story… according to Evan

Unfortunately, Evan was to be subjected to the regime of the same evil hag again the following year. He tried to escape, but his plans were foiled by the iron fist of his overlords. Evan's father said the evil hag would enjoy stewing Evan in the juices of a Garblaxian Fireworm. Evan was not fond of stew.

The evil hag continued to send cryptic notes to his parents:

Mr. and Ms. Doyle,

The Largellian Overlord wants to ingest your youngling.
Submit his culinary specifications before the cycle is out,
or your face will be forcibly removed.

Sincerely, Ms. H

That was okay. Evan didn't care for his parents' faces.

A few days later the evil hag ordered Evan to write a note. Evan
didn't want to, so he received sixty-seven lashes. Needless to say,
he wrote the note.

Dear Mom and Dad,

Ten thousand thundering typhoons! The evil aliens tried to corner and subdue me this morning, but I struck back, mounting a daring escape! But not before striking forceful blow after forceful blow upon those semaphoric anacoluthons! Vengeance is mine!

Sincerely, Evan

Unfortunately, the evil hag stapled another note to Evan's own. It was pink. Pink was not a color in Evan's parents' color spectrum. Accordingly, the sight of it sent them into a blind rage, similar to the Varxan Bulls on Hartakka IV.

The pink note, in which the evil hag's threats escalated, said:

> ### TEACHER REFERRAL
>
> Mr. and Ms. Doyle,
>
> Your youngling is out of control! Twelve of my minions were forcibly deactivated because of his insolence! He must be ingested immediately!
>
> Sincerely, Ms. H

Evan's parents spent the rest of the evening trying to gore him with their coiffures. He managed to sidestep his parents' continuous snorting and blind charging, and began plotting his next adventure.

CHAPTER 6

EVAN BRAIN *and His Babysitters*

Evan never minded when his parents traveled. And he didn't get tired of babysitters because they never came more than once. It was fun to have a new babysitter each time. His parents didn't seem as excited about this as he was.

When Evan was one, and his counterfeit sister and brother were two and three, a young man in seminary and his girlfriend spent the weekend at Evan's house. The young man had never taken care of children before. Evan thought he was nice. So was the young woman.

When his parents returned, his mother asked the seminary student how things went. After a long pause, he said, "I learned this weekend that kids are not for me."

Later Evan's father told his mother, "It's good to know our family is doing its part to keep the world population in check." Whatever that meant.

Evan had another nice babysitter named Sarah. He hoped she would come again.

His mother told him he needed to write Sarah a letter. So he did.

Dear Sarah,

I am sorry that I ignored you when you babysitted me. I will not sneak back outside when you tell me to go to my room. I will not do it again. I will also not slam things around or get in your way next time you babysit us.

Sincerely, Evan Doyle

Evan told Hobbes he thought Sarah would like his letter. But Sarah didn't come back. Maybe she wasn't used to kid superheroes.

Evan's favorite babysitter was his cousin Carrie. She let them watch TV nonstop when she wasn't playing Uno with them.

This didn't happen when his parents were home. Carrie was in the family so he knew he'd get to see her again.

This is the end of Eve's version of EVAN BRAIN and His Babysitters.

This is how EVAN BRAIN's brain viewed his babysitters.

EVAN BRAIN *and His Babysitters*
The Other Side of the Story… according to Evan

Every so often, Evan's parents left town, claiming they were going on one of his mother's business trips. But Evan saw right through their finely-crafted lies. He knew they ventured to committee hearings on the second moon of Galtrog Prime, in order to debrief their overseers about their plans for world domination.

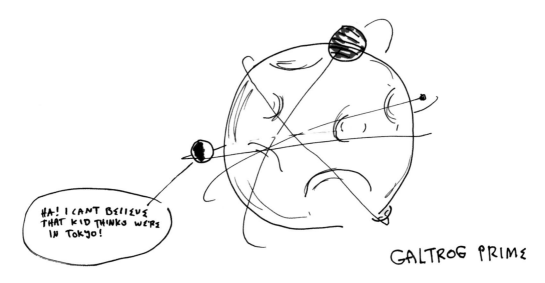

HA! I CANT BELIEVE THAT KID THINKS WE'RE IN TOKYO!

GALTROG PRIME

Evan used the opportunity to construct an elaborate plan to thwart them. Being wise to this, however, on every "vacation" Evan's parents sent in an assassin to "take care" of him. Each and every one Evan killed, with much aplomb.

When Evan was three-hundred-sixty-five cycles old, a mere larva, and his evil siblings were seven-hundred-thirty cycles old and one-thousand-ninety-five cycles old, a Rigellian with goat horns and a pointed tail was dispensed to watch over the young hatchlings. His mate was there, as well. Evan hated them both.

When Evan's parents returned, his mother asked the red-skinned Rigellian how things went. There was a long pause. Then the Rigellian said, "GWRRRK ARRRRK GLRRRRGARG BRRRRRG KRK GXZAP!"

Evan had another horrible sitter one August weekend while his parents were debriefing the Saartaarg Potentate on Venus. He hated her immensely. When his parents returned, his mother told him he needed to write Sarah a letter. So he did.

Dear Sarah,

I hate you.

Sincerely, Evan Doyle

Evan told Hobbes he thought Sarah would like his letter. But Sarah didn't come back.

Evan's favorite "sitter" was his cousin Carrie. She didn't stab him too hard.

EVAN BRAIN'S *Glossary of Weird Terms*

From the Other Side of the Story (presented in order of appearance)

1. EVAN BRAIN and His Family

Venusians — group of folk or creatures from Venus that stole the identities of Evan's family.

An Zargaxian Gortak from a distant galaxy — Evan's brother.

A Tentacle-eyed Bloodworm from the Sulfuric Mudpits of Rigel IV — Evan's sister.

2. EVAN BRAIN and the Comics

Orphax Jackalope — Evan likes to play chase with this mixed animal creature that jumps around a lot.

Eau de carcass and eau de gross — two bad-smelling colognes worn by Evan when he visits his grandmother.

Bulgari — a cologne that smells good.

Ixzam Toadstool — a poisonous mushroom from the province of Ixzam.

Ulgrog the Footstomper — an impatient, ill-tempered gladiator with whom Evan felt a close kinship.

3. EVAN BRAIN and His Kindergarten Teacher

Evil Torblax Mugtulla — Ms. M, Evan's kindergarten teacher who had a baby halfway through the school year.

A Gorbat — an ugly, dim-witted child who attacked Evan.

The evil overlord — Evan's school principal.

4. EVAN BRAIN and His First Grade Teacher

MWAAAHAHAHAHAHA! MWAAAHAHAHA! — Your son is driving me crazy.

O.'waplagh — "Insincerely, Evan"

5. EVAN BRAIN and His Second Grade Teacher

A Garblaxian Fireworm — Ms H, Evan's teacher, would have enjoyed stewing him in the juices of this repulsive worm.

The Largellian Overlord — hopes to eat Evan.

Semaphoric anacoluthons — the evil aliens, also known as the evil overlords from school, on whom Evan wreaks vengeance before escaping.

Varxan Bulls on Hartakka IV — go into a blind rage when they see pink (as do Evan's parents).

6. EVAN BRAIN and His Babysitters

Galtrog Prime — this planet, where Evan's parents went on his mother's business trips, has at least two moons. It is not Tokyo.

Three-hundred-sixty-five-cycles old — This is the Glatrog Prime method for expressng someone's age. A cycle is a day, so Evan was one. This explains why he is called a "mere larva".

Seven-hundred-thirty cycles — Evan's evil sister was two in earth years.

One-thousand-ninety-five cycles old — Evan's evil brother was three.

The red-skinned Rigellian with goat horns and the Rigellian's mate — Evan's seminarian babysitter and his girlfriend.

Saartaarg Potentate — the guy in charge on Venus.

EVAN BRAIN!

NOTES FROM THE AUTHORS

Dear Reader,

Thank you for purchasing our first book about Evan's nefarious antics. Now a few words about this, that and the other thing.

About his teachers...I'd like to thank Evan's teachers for their patience and forbearance. All are dedicated professionals who work hard to make a difference educating young people. I applaud their efforts and commitment.

About the book...the adventures I recount in EVAN BRAIN! are true stories. Some are embellished, but not much. The notes reproduced in the text are the real thing.

Evan wrote the parts entitled "The Other Side of the Story…According to Evan." I edited his work to make the copy flow and fit together with my sections, but in most cases not in any significant way. Evan favors the fantasy genre, which is evident in his fanciful renderings of the incidents.

About the drawings...the illustrations were a key challenge. For years now Evan, the family cartoonist, has claimed he cannot draw and refuses to illustrate his own work. Evan destroyed many of his earlier art projects when he decided he was not a fine artist. Evan remained stalwart that he would under no circumstances do the drawings for this book, or any other book, card or project.

I pointed out (to no avail) that neither Brian Andreas of StoryPeople fame nor Sandra Boynton can draw worth a flip either, but their clever and appealing work has achieved much popular acclaim and monetary success.

The matter was resolved when Evan determined he couldn't live without some kind of X-box thingee. We negotiated and he agreed to do the illustrations in exchange for the thingee. The imaginative drawings in this book are the delightful result.

By the time you read this, I expect Evan's brain cells will be seriously depleted from total mindless emersion in X-box-dom. X-boxing would not be at the top of my list for ways to spend one's time, but sometimes you have to strike a deal. I just hope Evan will have enough brain juice remaining to function on a daily basis and get a job at McDonald's.

Look for these stories in future volumes in the **EVAN BRAIN!** series:

"Evan and Quasimodo"
"Evan and His Christmas List"
"Evan and His Smarts"
"Evan and the Tooth Fairy"
"Evan and the Christmas Rat."

Sincerely,

Eve Becker-Doyle
The peaceful, hard-working, cruel, odd one

Dear Reader,

May you die a thousand deaths in the flaming mud pits of Ulkrack III.

Sincerely,

Evan "Brain" Doyle
The cool, smart, short, muscley one

OTHER SASSY CARTOONS
by EVAN BRAIN

Life's too short
to miss the good stuff!

Visit www.EVANBRAIN.com
for information about these
greeting and holiday cards

The Bing you really need
is a cherry in your Manhatten

Happy holidays!

Honey, I told you I only had
two pieces of gum, and I'm
saving the last one for Bobby.

But that one's not Bobby's.
It's mine!
I already chewed Bobby's.

Get what's coming to you.

Who does your baby look like?

It's uncanny...but there's a
remarkable resemblance
to my wife's old boyfriend.

This one's gonna look like you!
Congratulations on your new baby.

Folks say I'm hard to ignore,
but it's well worth the effort.

(blank)

and his sister Tory!

*Fashion Statement
Class with Sass*

Only 143 shopping days until my birthday!

But today it's
all about you!

Happy birthday!

Season's greetings

The holidays are a time to be with
family and those you love...
    Come to think of it, maybe this year
    you ought to plan a trip to Tahiti.

When your doctor
tells you
to lose weight...
you know
what to do.

Change doctors.

Sick and tired?

Or just tired?

Up and at 'em,
you worthless malingerer!

Still together?

These days that's
something worth celebrating.

Happy anniversary.

QUICK ORDER FORM

🖥️	**Online orders**	www.evanbrain.com
🖱️	**E-mail orders**	orders@evanbrain.com
⌨️	**Fax orders**	214.350.9275
✉️	**Postal orders**	Becker Doyle & Assoc. PO Box 541715, Dallas, TX 75354-1715

Item	Qty	Price	Amount
EVAN BRAIN! **Book**		$13.95	
EVAN BRAIN! **Audio CD**		$11.95	

Subtotal	

Shipping
$ 4.75 for first book
  2.00 ea. add'l book
  4.75 for first CD
  2.00 ea. add'l CD	

Gift wrap $3.00 per book	
Subtotal	
In Texas add 8.25%	
Total	

Method of Payment   *Please do not send cash*

☐ Visa   ☐ Mastercard

☐ Check/Money Order (Please write steet address on check. PO Box is not acceptable.)

☐☐☐☐ ☐☐☐☐ ☐☐☐☐ ☐☐☐☐   ☐☐-☐☐

Account Number   Expiration Date

Cardholder Signature _____

Name_____ Phone (___)_____

E-mail Address _____

Shipping Address _____

City/State/Zip _____

Ask about EVAN BRAIN *action figures!*